A Note From Rick Renner

I am on a personal quest to see a "revival of the Bible" so people can establish their lives on a firm foundation that will stand strong and endure the test when the end-time storm winds begin to intensify.

In order to experience a revival of the Bible in your personal life, it is important to take time each day to read, receive, and apply its truths to your life. James tells us that if we will continue in the perfect law of liberty — refusing to be forgetful hearers but determined to be doers — we will be blessed in our ways. As you watch or listen to the programs in this series and work through this corresponding study guide, I trust that you will search the Scriptures and allow the Holy Spirit to help you hear something new from God's Word that applies specifically to your life. I encourage you to be a doer of the Word that He reveals to you. Whatever the cost, I assure you — it will be worth it.

> Thy words were found, and I did eat them;
> and thy word was unto me the joy and rejoicing of mine heart:
> for I am called by thy name, O Lord God of hosts.
> — Jeremiah 15:16

Your brother and friend in Jesus Christ,

Rick Renner

Rick Renner

Pastoral Ministry

Copyright © 2020 by Rick Renner
8316 E. 73rd St.
Tulsa, Oklahoma 74133

Published by Rick Renner Ministries
www.renner.org

ISBN 13: 978-1-68031-764-0

eBook ISBN 13: 978-1-68031-765-7

How To Use This Study Guide

This five-lesson study guide corresponds to *"Pastoral Ministry" With Rick Renner* (Renner TV). Each lesson in this study guide covers a topic that is addressed during the program series, with questions and references supplied to draw you deeper into your own private study of the Scriptures on this subject.

To derive the most benefit from this study guide, consider the following:

First, watch or listen to the program prior to working through the corresponding lesson in this guide. (Programs can also be viewed at **renner.org** by clicking on the Media/Archives links.)

Second, take the time to look up the scriptures included in each lesson. Prayerfully consider their application to your own life.

Third, use a journal or notebook to make note of your answers to each lesson's Study Questions and Practical Application challenges.

Fourth, invest specific time in prayer and in the Word of God to consult with the Holy Spirit. Write down the scriptures or insights He reveals to you.

Finally, take action! Whatever the Lord tells you to do according to His Word, do it.

For added insights on this subject, it is recommended that you obtain Rick Renner's book *Chosen by God*. You may also select from Rick's other available resources by placing your order at **renner.org** or by calling 1-800-742-5593.

TOPIC

Statistics About Pastors

SCRIPTURES

1. **Ephesians 4:11,12** — And he gave some, apostles; and some, prophets; and some, evangelists; and some, pastors and teachers; for the perfecting of the saints, for the work of the ministry, for the edifying of the body of Christ.

2. **1 Peter 1:16** — Because it is written, Be ye holy; for I am holy.

GREEK WORDS

1. "pastors" — ποιμήν (*poimen*): a shepherd; pictures one who tends, rules, governs, feeds, guards, guides, and protects a flock

SYNOPSIS

The five lessons in this study on *Pastoral Ministry* will focus on the following topics:

- Statistics About Pastors
- God's Expectations of Pastors
- God's Specific Charge to Pastors
- God's Reward for Pastors
- God's Choice for a Pastor To Feed You

The emphasis of this lesson:

Discover some of the most recent statistics and trends regarding those in pastoral ministry. From the hours they keep to providing for their families to living up to the demands and expectations of others, today's pastors are surrounded by many challenges that are really taking their toll.

In order to build, strengthen, and advance the Kingdom of God in the earth, Jesus gave the Church the fivefold ministry gifts. The apostle Paul described these gifts, and the purpose for them, in Ephesians 4:11 and 12, stating, "And he [Jesus] gave some, apostles; and some, prophets; and some, evangelists; and some, pastors and teachers; for the perfecting of the saints, for the work of the ministry, for the edifying of the body of Christ."

The word "pastors" in verse 11 is the Greek word *poimen*, which is the very word for *a shepherd*, and it pictures *one who tends, rules, governs, feeds, guards, guides, and protects a flock*. A better translation of this verse would be, "And he [Jesus] gave some, apostles; and some, prophets; and some, evangelists; and some, *to be shepherds* and teachers."

This brings us to a few important questions: How much do you know and understand about the job of your pastor? What kind of schedule is he required to keep? What demands and expectations are on him and his family? Does he have many friends? And how likely is he to actually retire from ministry and enjoy financial peace in his golden years of life? Here is a sobering look at the answers to these questions.

CURRENT STATISTICS ABOUT PASTORS

After questioning a cross-section of pastors in the Western world, here are the latest statistics and trends we are seeing in pastoral ministry. Of all the statistics, the first one is encouraging, and it says that 93 percent of pastors feel privileged to be called to pastoral ministry. As inspiring and upbeat as this attitude may be, it is overshadowed by the data regarding a pastor's workload and the overall conditions he or she is facing.

Work and Personal Time

- 72% of pastors say they work between 55 to 75 hours per week. Indeed, it takes plenty of concentration and hard work to do pastoral ministry.

- 84% of pastors feel they are on call 24/7. When you are a pastor, people in the congregation want — and feel they need — to have access to you around the clock.

- 65% of pastors feel they have not taken enough vacation time with their family over the last five years. What's even worse, 28% of pastors report feeling guilty for taking personal time off.

- 78% of pastors report having their vacation and personal time interrupted with ministry duties or expectations. The truth is few pastors take breaks that are not interrupted by a crisis of some kind. Whether it is a marriage suddenly on the brink of divorce or the church being flooded by water from broken pipes, it seems that a pastor's work is never done.

Living Up to People's Demands and Expectations

- 48% of pastors agree they often feel the demands of ministry are greater than they can handle. This number likely reflects the lack of a team to help lighten the load and not enough teaching on how to lead and delegate responsibility.

- 35% of pastors report the demands of the church deny them from spending time with their family. To remedy this, pastors need to learn how to structure regular time with their family as well as time alone with their spouse.

- 66% of pastors report that church members expect a minister and his family to live at a higher moral standard than themselves. Although pastors are called to set a high standard, they are not the only ones. All believers are called to live holy lives (*see* 1 Peter 1:16).

- 52% of pastors feel overworked and that they cannot meet their church's unrealistic expectations of them, which is closely connected with the fact that 54% of pastors find the role of a pastor to be over-whelming.

- 80% of pastors have felt unqualified and discouraged in their role as pastor at least one or more times in their ministry. This is why pastors need to build into their schedule opportunities for continued learning. Regular times of personal study will help ensure that they are spiritually equipped and never stop growing.

Conflicts, Crises, and Personal Attacks

- 75% of pastors report a significant stress-related crisis at least once in their ministry. There are a number of pastors who experience multiple crises of this nature.

- 40% of pastors report a serious conflict with a parishioner at least once in the last year, and 33% of pastors report they have experienced a significant personal attack at their church.

- 80% of pastors will need to confront conflict in their church in the future. Like it or not, when you're the pastor of the church, sometimes you have to deal with difficult situations, and your actions are sometimes misunderstood. People begin to question you and think things like, *Pastor really could have responded better than that. I just don't understand why he did what he did.* Of course the enemy is also at work, relentlessly firing thoughts of accusation, criticism, and doubt at the minds of church members. With these forces in operation, it is easy to see how a pastor will have to deal with some kind of a personal attack or another conflict in the church. Dealing with situations of this nature can cause great stress, which is why one of the best things you can do for your pastor is to pray for him and his family.

Feeling Isolated, Alone, and Afraid

- 53% of pastors are often concerned about their family's financial security. Unfortunately, many pastors are not paid appropriately. In fact, several of them work a secular job in addition to carrying out their pastoral duties — just to make sure ends meet. Furthermore, many pastors have no retirement plan and don't know what they're going to do when they reach retirement age.

- 35% of pastors battle depression or feelings of inadequacy, which is sad but understandable, given the long work hours, little-to-no personal and family time, and multiple concerns a pastor faces regarding the church as well as personal issues.

- 70% of pastors report that they do not have someone they consider to be a close friend. Taking this figure into account, it is no wonder that 33% of pastors report feeling isolated in their position, and 27% of pastors report not having anyone to turn to for help in a crisis situation. The truth is, it is very difficult for the person leading the church to find someone he or she can trust and can turn to for help in times of trouble. This is why it is crucial for pastors to build and maintain a network of healthy relationships consisting of like-minded people with whom they feel safe to share their hearts.

- 70% of pastors report they have a lower self-image now than when they first started in ministry. When they began, their hearts were filled with hope and great expectations; they believed many people were behind them and wanted them to succeed. But over time as the stressors of the job grew, personal and family time evaporated, and they became spiritually depleted, fatigue and fear set in, drastically reducing their self-image.

The Exhaustion Factor

- 57% of pastors feel fulfilled and that it is a privilege to be a pastor. At the same time, however, they are discouraged, stressed, and fatigued in their position.

- 50% or more of pastors are unhealthy, overweight, and do not exercise. If you think about it, pastors are in many meetings where they are inundated by food. Considering the long hours and other stressors that come with ministry, many pastors feel overeating and not exercising are unavoidable, but that is not true. With the empowerment of the Holy Spirit and the establishment of some personal discipline, one can gain control over his eating and insert exercise into his routine.

- 26% of pastors report being over fatigued, which is directly connected with their workload and the stressors that come with the position. Again, learning to schedule personal time and vacation time will go a long way to reduce this number and many other negative statistics.

- 28% of pastors report they are spiritually undernourished, which is really sad. However, in most cases, the fault lies primarily with the pastor. If he will take responsibility and feed himself spiritually, the feelings of undernourishment will greatly dissipate. Anyone who consistently gives out to others must replenish himself or they *will* run dry.

- 71% of churches have no plan for their pastor to receive a periodic sabbatical, which is very concerning. When a pastor is serving day in and day out — not only preparing and delivering sermons, but also visiting people in the hospital, counseling individuals and couples, and overseeing all aspects of the ministry — he needs a regular sabbatical to be personally refreshed, renewed, and refilled.

What Are the Results of These Statistics?

Some of the most alarming and disheartening statistics are the ones you are about to read. The first one is that every month, 250 pastors leave the ministry and never return. What's more, only 1 out of every 10 pastors will actually retire as a pastor. Said another way, 90 percent of everyone who enters pastoral ministry will quit before they reach retirement age. Only 10 percent of all pastors will make it all the way to the end.

Think about it. Every Sunday you go to church and enjoy the opportunity to enter into worship and then sit and hear the message your pastor has prepared. But you probably never realized the weight of all the challenges and pressures he is facing. At the same time he is encouraging you to walk in faith and make godly choices, he has to make those same choices himself — and many others that you will likely never face. These sobering statistics are not meant to instill guilt, but to cultivate a new appreciation for your pastor and motivate you to regularly pray for him and his family. He truly is a gift from God to help you grow and mature in your relationship with Jesus.

In our next lesson, we will look at what God's expectations are of pastors, including seven specific duties He has called them to carry out as the shepherd of your church.

STUDY QUESTIONS

Study to shew thyself approved unto God, a workman that needeth not to be ashamed, rightly dividing the word of truth.
— 2 Timothy 2:15

1. Pastors truly are a gift from God, and it is important that you get to know yours. Stop and think:

    • *What is your pastor's name and the name of his spouse and children (if he has any)?*

    • *How did he come to know the Lord? When and how did he sense God calling him into ministry?*

    • *When it comes to leading your church family, what does your pastor enjoy most about his job? What burdens him and causes the greatest concern?*

    • *What is he strongly praying and believing God to do in your church? How about in your community?*

PRACTICAL APPLICATION

But be ye doers of the word, and not hearers only, deceiving your own selves.
— James 1:22

1. After hearing and reading through all of the data that was presented, what is your initial, personal reaction? How does it move your heart with compassion for your pastor?

2. Of all the statistics about pastors in ministry, which is most concerning to you? Why? What practical steps might you take to lovingly help alleviate this pressure?

3. Be honest. Which statement would you say better describes your thoughts and conversations about your pastor in the privacy of your home:

   • *I am one of my pastor's greatest supporters and cheerleaders. I look to believe the best about him and the decisions he makes.*

   OR

   • *I am one of my pastor's greatest critics. I don't think he's doing a very good job, and many times I struggle to trust him and believe the best about him.*

4. In light of the statement you chose, is there a mindset or attitude you need to repent of and ask God for forgiveness?

LESSON 2

TOPIC
God's Expectations of Pastors

SCRIPTURES

1. **Ephesians 4:11** — And he gave some, apostles; and some, prophets; and some, evangelists; and some, pastors and teachers.

2. **Ezekiel 34:1-12,14-16** — And the word of the Lord came unto me, saying, Son of man, prophesy against the shepherds of Israel, prophesy, and say unto them, Thus saith the Lord God unto the shepherds; Woe be to the shepherds of Israel that do feed themselves! should not the shepherds feed the flocks? Ye eat the fat, and ye clothe you with the wool, ye kill them that are fed: but ye feed not the flock. The diseased have ye not strengthened, neither have ye healed that which was sick, neither have ye bound up that which was broken, neither have ye brought again that which was driven away, neither have ye

sought that which was lost; but with force and with cruelty have ye ruled them. And they were scattered, because there is no shepherd.... My sheep wandered through all the mountains, and upon every high hill: yea, my flock was scattered upon all the face of the earth, and none did search or seek after them. Therefore, ye shepherds, hear the word of the Lord, As I live, saith the Lord God, surely because my flock became a prey, and my flock became meat to every beast of the field, because there was no shepherd, neither did my shepherds search for my flock, but the shepherds fed themselves, and fed not my flock; Therefore, O ye shepherds, hear the word of the Lord; Thus saith the Lord God; Behold, I am against the shepherds; and I will require my flock at their hand, and cause them to cease from feeding the flock; neither shall the shepherds feed themselves any more; for I will deliver my flock from their mouth, that they may not be meat for them. For thus saith the Lord God; Behold, I, even I, will both search my sheep, and seek them out. As a shepherd seeketh out his flock in the day that he is among his sheep that are scattered; so will I seek out my sheep, and [I] will deliver them out of all places where they have been scattered in the cloudy and dark day. ...I will feed them in a good pasture, and upon the high mountains of Israel shall their fold be: there shall they lie in a good fold, and in a fat pasture shall they feed upon the mountains of Israel. I will feed my flock, and I will cause them to lie down, saith the Lord God. I will seek that which was lost, and bring again that which was driven away, and will bind up that which was broken, and will strengthen that which was sick: but I will destroy the fat and the strong; I will feed them with judgment.

GREEK WORDS

1. "pastors" — ποιμήν (*poimen*): a shepherd; pictures one who tends, rules, governs, feeds, guards, guides, and protects a flock

SYNOPSIS

In our first lesson, we learned some sobering statistics about pastors and the myriad of challenges they face as they serve in ministry. We also saw that they are one of the fivefold ministry gifts Christ gave the Church. In Ephesians 4:11, our anchor verse, it says, "And he [Jesus] gave some, apostles; and some, prophets; and some, evangelists; and some, pastors and teachers."

In Greek, the word for "pastors" is the word *poimen*, which is the word for "shepherds." It pictures *one who tends, rules, governs, feeds, guards, guides, and protects a flock.* The truth is pastors are shepherds of people. They have been equipped by Christ — the Good Shepherd (*see* John 10:11) — to continue the work He began, which is to tend, feed, govern, guide, guard, and protect the people entrusted to their care.

The emphasis of this lesson:

Ezekiel 34:1-16 gives us a clear picture of God's expectations of pastors. First and foremost, above all other duties, pastors are called by God to regularly feed the congregation they oversee with the pure truth of God's Word.

A Clear, Biblical Picture of What Pastors Are To Do

In Ezekiel 34, God spoke some very strong words of correction to the shepherds of Israel. Apparently, these spiritual leaders were extremely deficient in fulfilling their responsibilities. As we read through God's reprimand, we can see clearly what He expects a shepherd — or pastor — to do by what He corrected the shepherds of Israel for *not* doing.

Ezekiel 34:1-3 says, "And the word of the Lord came unto me, saying, Son of man, prophesy against the shepherds of Israel, prophesy, and say unto them, Thus saith the Lord God unto the shepherds; Woe be to the shepherds of Israel that do feed themselves! should not the shepherds feed the flocks? Ye eat the fat, and ye clothe you with the wool, ye kill them that are fed: but ye feed not the flock."

It is interesting to note that twice in these three verses, God corrected the shepherds for not "feeding the flocks." He mentions this again and again throughout the chapter, which tells us that **the primary responsibility of a pastor (shepherd) is to provide spiritual nourishment for the congregation (sheep)**. God is not against a pastor feeding and clothing himself or being blessed. But He is against pastors only being concerned for their own needs and not doing what He has called them to do.

God went on to say, "The diseased have ye not strengthened, neither have ye healed that which was sick, neither have ye bound up that which was broken, neither have ye brought again that which was driven away, neither have ye sought that which was lost; but with force and with cruelty have ye ruled them" (Ezekiel 34:4). Here we see five specific things the shepherds of Israel had *failed* to do:

1. **The diseased ye have not strengthened.**
2. **Neither have ye healed that which was sick.**
3. **Neither have ye bound up that which was broken.**
4. **Neither have ye brought again that which was driven away.**
5. **Neither have ye sought that which was lost.**

By hearing what these shepherds — or pastors — were *not* doing, we can determine what pastors *should* be doing.

1. **Pastors are to strengthen the diseased.** This means pastors are to nurture, encourage, and strengthen those who are struggling with issues of sin or any other area of their life. There are many in the Church who are diseased, and pastors are to do all they can to make them whole. It is the teaching of God's Word that brings wholeness.

2. **Pastors are to heal those who are sick.** The word "sick" here can refer to those who are physically or spiritually ill. In every church there are people who are spiritually sick and physically sick. Pastors have a responsibility to help bring healing to people who are sick in their souls and bodies. The correct teaching of the Bible and ministry of the Holy Spirit will bring about the healing of those who are sick.

3. **Pastors are to bind up those who are broken.** Sheep have a propensity to get hurt and even break a leg. It was the responsibility of the shepherd to make splints for the wounded sheep and help them heal. In the same way, pastors have a God-given responsibility to bind up people who are broken by life — broken in their marriage, their relationships, or their finances — and help them mend. The Word of God is like a splint that brings correction and restoration to those who are broken or fractured in any area of their lives.

4. **Pastors are to bring back those who were driven away.** There are many people who experience hurt in church. In fact, millions of wounded Christians do not attend church. They don't understand why things happened the way they did or why certain decisions were made, and they become disappointed or offended and leave. Rather than say, "Good riddance," pastors have a level of responsibility to go after and find people who have wandered away and encourage them back into the congregation.

5. **Pastors are to seek those who are lost.** There are people in the church as well as outside the church who are lost. Although pastors are not evangelists, they do have a God-given responsibility to lead their church to reach out and make every effort to rescue those who are without Christ and are perishing.

After God pointed out all the areas where the shepherds of Israel were falling short, He told them "…with force and with cruelty have ye ruled them [the people of Israel]" (Ezekiel 34:4). Although God is not against pastors leading and ruling the congregations for which they are responsible, He is against them neglecting or abusing His people.

What Happens to Pastors
Who Refuse To Do Their Job?

God continued to correct the shepherds of Israel by saying, "And they were scattered, because there is no shepherd…. My sheep wandered through all the mountains, and upon every high hill: yea, my flock was scattered upon all the face of the earth, and none did search or seek after them" (Ezekiel 34:5,6).

The reason the "sheep" had wandered off was because the shepherds were not doing their job. To make matters worse, the shepherds failed to go after the ones who were scattered. This tells us that when pastoral leadership is deficient, people begin to wander off into wrong places. However, when there is strong pastoral leadership, it helps hold the "flock" together.

Speaking through the prophet Ezekiel, God went on to say, "Therefore, ye shepherds, hear the word of the Lord; As I live, saith the Lord God, surely because my flock became a prey, and my flock became meat to every beast of the field, because there was no shepherd, neither did my shepherds search for my flock, but the shepherds fed themselves, and fed not my flock; Therefore, O ye shepherds, hear the word of the Lord; Thus saith the Lord God; Behold, I am against the shepherds; and I will require my flock at their hand, and cause them to cease from feeding the flock; neither shall the shepherds feed themselves any more; for I will deliver my flock from their mouth, that they may not be meat for them" (Ezekiel 34:7-10).

Twice more in these verses, God scolded the shepherds of Israel for not feeding His sheep and only feeding themselves — punctuating the fact that **the primary responsibility of a pastor (shepherd) is to spiritually nourish the congregation with the teaching of Scripture.** For their continued irresponsibility, God said He was against them and would take the flock out of their keeping.

God Promises To Be a Shepherd to Those Being Neglected

Once God called attention to the shortcomings of the shepherds of Israel, He made an amazing promise to the sheep that had been ignored and abandoned:

"For thus saith the Lord God; Behold, I, even I, will both search my sheep, and seek them out. As a shepherd seeketh out his flock in the day that he is among his sheep that are scattered; so will I seek out my sheep, and [I] will deliver them out of all places where they have been scattered in the cloudy and dark day. I will feed them in a good pasture, and upon the high mountains of Israel shall their fold be: there shall they lie in a good fold, and in a fat pasture shall they feed upon the mountains of Israel. I will feed my flock, and I will cause them to lie down, saith the Lord God. I will seek that which was lost, and bring again that which was driven away, and will bind up that which was broken, and will strengthen that which was sick: but I will destroy the fat and the strong; I will feed them with judgment" (Ezekiel 34:11,12,14-16).

In these five verses, the Lord tells the irresponsible shepherds, "If you won't do the job of pastoring My people, I will do it Myself! I Myself will strengthen the diseased, heal those that are sick, bind up those that are broken, bring again those that have been driven away, and seek out those that are lost. I'm going to bring My sheep — My people — into a good, safe pasture where they can lie down in a good fold without fear."

Every good pastor should desire and aim at feeding and protecting the spiritual flock that has been entrusted to him. He should also seek to lead them into "high places," which signifies bringing them into new, higher spiritual levels. Likewise, he should allow them to "lie down," enabling them to feel safe and secure. This is the heart of God for His people.

Christ gave the Church "pastors" — the Greek word *poimen* — to serve as shepherds of His sheep. Every pastor is to be *a provider, a protector,* and *a ruler of their local congregation.* They have been entrusted by God with a very high position and given the responsibility to care for God's people in these specific ways. As we wrap up this lesson, here are seven specific duties of a good pastor:

Seven Duties of a Good Shepherd for His Sheep

1. He knows the state of his sheep (or congregation).
2. He knows how to nourish, feed, and reprove the sheep to bring them into a state of spiritual soundness.
3. He knows how to rescue and restore the sheep who have fallen into sin.
4. He knows how to find the sheep who have been driven away.
5. He knows how to bring sheep back into the fold who have strayed into strange pastures.
6. He knows how to oppose and expel wolves who have gotten in among the sheep and are scattering them from each other and from God.
7. He knows how to preach, explain, and defend the truth for the sheep.

These are the seven expectations God has for every pastor. In our next lesson, we will see God's specific charge to pastors outlined in Acts 20:28.

STUDY QUESTIONS

> Study to shew thyself approved unto God, a workman that
> needeth not to be ashamed, rightly dividing the word of truth.
> — 2 Timothy 2:15

1. As part of the fivefold ministry gifts, pastors are vital to the spiritual growth and health of the Church. Prior to this lesson, how did you envision the role of a pastor? How has your understanding been expanded and/or redirected?
2. Take time to reread Ezekiel 34:11,12,14-16, which highlights God's promise to be a Shepherd to those being neglected. How is He personally encouraging you with His words in this passage?
3. Carefully reflect on the seven duties of a good pastor (shepherd). Of these seven, which ones describe the way your pastor has been used by God to shepherd *you*? Briefly describe a meaningful situation in which your pastor's care was a huge blessing in your life.

PRACTICAL APPLICATION

**But be ye doers of the word, and not hearers only,
deceiving your own selves.
— James 1:22**

1. There are many people who have experienced hurt in church. In fact, millions of wounded Christians do not attend church any longer. Does this describe you? Did something happened to you (or someone you know) in a church you previously attended that disappointed or offended you? If so, briefly describe what took place.

2. It is no accident that you're doing this study and this situation of offense has been brought back to your memory. God wants to heal you — *right now* — and bring you back into a healthy fellowship with Him and other believers. All you need to do is pray a simple prayer like this:

Father, thank You for loving me so much that You don't want to leave me wounded. Please forgive me for holding onto this hurt/offense. I release [say the person's name] *into Your hands. You are the Judge, not me. You have forgiven me of so many things, and You want me to forgive others* (*see* Matthew 6:14,15). *With Your strength, I choose to forgive* [say the person's name] *and I choose to bless* [say the person's name] *just as You instructed us to do* (*see* 1 Peter 3:9,10). *Please heal the hurts in my heart and restore Your peace and joy. In Jesus' Name, Amen.*

LESSON 3

TOPIC

God's Specific Charge to Pastors

SCRIPTURES

1. **Ephesians 4:11,12** — And he gave some, apostles; and some, prophets; and some, evangelists; and some, pastors and teachers; for the perfecting of the saints, for the work of the ministry, for the edifying of the body of Christ.

2. **Acts 20:28** — Take heed therefore unto yourselves, and to all the flock, over the which the Holy Ghost hath made you overseers, to feed the church of God, which he hath purchased with his own blood.

GREEK WORDS

1. "pastors" — **ποιμήν** (*poimen*): a shepherd; pictures one who tends, rules, governs, feeds, guards, guides, and protects a flock

2. "take heed" — **προσέχω** (*prosecho*): to give one's full attention to what is being spoken and heard and to draw as near to it as possible; to give one's full attention

3. "all" — **πα ντὶ** (*panti*): each and every part; all inclusive; no one excluded or missing

4. "flock" — **ποίμνιον** (*poimnion*): a flock of sheep; a congregation

5. "hath made" — **τίθημι** (*tithemi*): to set in place; to position; to fix; to establish

6. "overseers" — **ἐπίσκοπος** (*episkopos*): to look over; oversight; to administrate or manage; pictures a supervisory position; one whose responsibility is to guide, direct, and give oversight

7. "feed" — **ποιμαίνω** (*poimaino*): to shepherd; to tend; to rule; to govern; pictures feeding, guarding, guiding, and protecting a flock

8. "church" — **ἐκκλησία** (*ekklesia*): a called, separated, and prestigious assembly; an assembly of distinguished citizens; to be selected from society and invited to join this assembly was a great honor; in the New Testament, depicts the body of believers who have been called out, called forth, selected, and assembled to be God's representatives in every town, city, state or nation; a body called to make decisions that affect the atmosphere of a region

9. "purchased" — **περιποιέω** (*peripoieo*): pictures a comprehensive purchase; total purchase; completely purchased and taken wholly

SYNOPSIS

In our last lesson, we looked at God's reprimand of the shepherds of Israel in Ezekiel 34. By reading His rebuke of the responsibilities they were neglecting, we can determine what a shepherd — or pastor — is supposed to do. God's expectations of pastors are very clear in this passage, and when they fail to do their job, He Himself is against them, which is not a place any of us wants to be.

Remember, pastors are one of the fivefold ministry gifts Jesus gave to the Church. The apostle Paul described this in his letter to the church of Ephesus, saying, "And he [Jesus] gave some, apostles; and some, prophets; and some, evangelists; and some, pastors and teachers; for the perfecting of the saints, for the work of the ministry, for the edifying of the body of Christ" (Ephesians 4:11,12).

We saw that the word "pastor" in verse 11 is the Greek word *poimen*, which is the very word for *a shepherd*. It pictures *one who tends, rules, governs, feeds, guards, guides, and protects a flock*. A better translation of this verse would be, "And he [Jesus] gave some, apostles; and some, prophets; and some, evangelists; and some, *to be shepherds* and teachers." Again, as we have noted, the primary task of every pastor is to feed the congregation he oversees with the truth of God's Word.

The emphasis of this lesson:

Pastors are selected by the Holy Spirit to oversee the most prestigious people on the planet — the Church. They are to first feed themselves and care for their spiritual needs; then they are to feed and care for the spiritual needs of God's people entrusted to them.

The Seven Duties of a Good Pastor

We concluded our previous lesson by quickly noting seven specific responsibilities of a shepherd or pastor. **A good pastor knows…**

1. The state of his sheep (or congregation).
2. How to nourish, feed, and reprove the sheep to bring them into a state of spiritual soundness.
3. How to rescue and restore the sheep who have fallen into sin.
4. How to find the sheep who have been driven away. Oftentimes, believers don't understand why certain things happened and they become offended with someone in the church and leave. A good pastor knows how to find those who have left the fellowship and bring them back.
5. How to bring sheep back into the fold who have strayed into strange pastures. Sometimes believers get off into strange teaching, and a good pastor has the responsibility to bring them back into the fold and begin feeding them the Word again.

6. How to oppose and expel wolves who have gotten in among the sheep and are scattering them from each other and from God.
7. How to preach, explain, and defend the truth for the sheep.

Indeed, there is much responsibility when it comes to pastoral ministry. This divine calling to tend, feed, rule, govern, guard, guide and protect is vital to the health of the church and individual believers.

Pastors Are To 'Take Heed' to Themselves First Then the Flock

When we come to Acts 20:28, we see the apostle Paul is speaking to the elders, or pastors, of the church of Ephesus, explaining God's specific charge to them. He said, "Take heed therefore unto yourselves, and to all the flock, over the which the Holy Ghost hath made you overseers, to feed the church of God, which he hath purchased with his own blood." Once again we see the chief responsibility of pastors is *to feed the people of God*.

But also observe the words "take heed." In Greek, it is the word *prosecho*, which is a compound of the word *pros*, meaning *to turn*, and the word *echo*, meaning *to embrace*. When the two words are combined, the new word *prosecho* means *giving one's full attention to what is being spoken and heard and drawing as near to it as possible*. It depicts *a person giving his or her full attention to a matter and embracing what is said.* Therefore, when Paul said, "take heed," he didn't just ask the pastors in Ephesus to *listen*. He urged them to throw back their shoulders, hold their heads high, open their ears, and give their entire attention to what he was saying.

Specifically, Paul said, "Take heed therefore unto *yourselves...*" (Acts 20:28). The first responsibility of any spiritual leader is to take notice of and pay attention to himself. If a pastor doesn't feed himself healthy spiritual food, he will be malnourished and unable to adequately feed his congregation. If he is not hearing from God and growing, how can he help someone else? He needs a daily discipline of praying, reading, and studying the Bible. Likewise, if he isn't taking care of his body — which is the temple of the Holy Spirit (*see* 1 Corinthians 3:16) — he won't be around very long to minister to others. Hence, the first personal responsibility of any spiritual leader, including a pastor, is to take heed to himself.

Once this priority is being managed, a pastor is then ready to turn his attention to "all the flock." The word "all" is the Greek word *panti*, which is an all-inclusive term, meaning *each and every part; no one excluded or missing*. In other words, the pastor is responsible for *every person* who is a member of the "flock" or *congregation* — not just the ones he likes.

Pastors Are God-Appointed — Not Self-Appointed

Paul went on to say that pastors are to care for "…all the flock, over the which the Holy Ghost hath made [them] overseers…" (Acts 20:28). The phrase "hath made" is a translation of the Greek word *tithemi*, which means *to set in place; to position; to fix*; or *to establish*. The use of this word tells us that pastors have been *set in place* and *fixed in position* by the Holy Spirit; they are not self-appointed. As a result, they are accountable directly to the Holy Spirit for the way they do their jobs.

Unlike other occupations, being a pastor is a calling from God that lasts a lifetime. It is not an optional career one haphazardly chooses. The Bible states that the Holy Spirit handpicks individuals to serve as pastors in the Church, and they are answerable to Him as "overseers."

The word "overseers" is the Greek word *episkopos*, which is a compound of the word *epi*, meaning *over*, and the word *skopos*, meaning *to look*. *Skopos* is from where we get the words *microscope* and *telescope*, which describe instruments used to look at things. When the words *epi* and *skopos* are combined to form *episkopos*, it means *to look over, to administrate*, or *to manage*. It pictures *a supervisory position* or *one whose responsibility it is to guide, direct, and give oversight*. Moreover, it is the word that describes *a bishop or an overseer*.

Again, it is the Holy Spirit who chooses the individuals He desires to serve as supervisors, managers, and administrators of the local churches. Although a pastor is not called to do everything in the church, as an *episkopos*, he is the one responsible to make sure everything in the church is getting done. Indeed, the buck stops with him. Ultimately, God will hold pastors responsible for what happens in the congregation they are overseeing.

Pastors Are Privileged To Oversee
the Most Prestigious People on the Planet

Looking again at Acts 20:28, Paul said, "Take heed therefore unto your-selves, and to all the flock, over the which the Holy Ghost hath made you overseers, to feed the church of God, which he hath purchased with his own blood." Just as we saw in Ezekiel 34, we see again that the primary responsibility of pastors is to "feed the church of God...."

The word "feed" is the Greek word *poimaino*, which means *to shepherd, to tend, to rule,* or *to govern.* It pictures *feeding, guarding, guiding, and protecting a flock.* The most beneficial thing a pastor can do for his church is to feed them the pure and powerful Word of God. Feasting on the Word enables people to recognize error in their lives, discern what is right and wrong, and recognize the voice of the Holy Spirit. Through the knowledge and application of the Word, people are transformed into the likeness of Jesus and experience divine health. There is no substitute for God's Word.

Through Paul, God said pastors are to "feed the church of God." The Greek word for "church" here is *ekklesia.* It is a compound of the word *ek,* which means *out,* and the word *klesia,* from the word *kaleo,* meaning *to call.* When the two words are compounded, they form the word *ekklesia* — the word for "church," the *called out ones.*

What's interesting about this word is that it did not originate in Scripture but was borrowed from the Athenian culture. It described *a called, separated, and prestigious assembly; a prestigious assembly of distinguished citizens who determined laws, debated public policy, formulated new policies, argued and ruled in judicial matters, elected the chief magistrates of the land, and decided who should be banished.* To be selected from society and invited to join this assembly was a great honor.

In the New Testament, it depicts *the body of believers who have been called out, called forth, selected, and assembled to be God's representatives in every town, city, state or nation; a body called to make decisions that affect the atmosphere of the region in which they lived.* Furthermore, these *called out ones* (the Church) have been "...purchased with his own blood" (Acts 20:28). The word "purchased" is from the Greek word *peripoieo,* and it pictures *a comprehensive or total purchase; completely purchased and taken wholly.*

The point is that when pastors grow weary and become frustrated working with people, they must remember that it is an honor to be a pastor. They have been uniquely selected by the Holy Spirit as an overseer — to manage, supervise, and administrate the Church, which is not just any group of people. It is the most prestigious group of individuals on the face of the earth. They have been *wholly* purchased with the blood of Jesus and called out by God to make decisions that affect the atmosphere of the regions in which they live.

In our next lesson, we will talk more about God's charge to pastors and examine the reward He promises to the shepherds who faithfully carry out their calling.

STUDY QUESTIONS

Study to shew thyself approved unto God, a workman that needeth not to be ashamed, rightly dividing the word of truth.
— 2 Timothy 2:15

1. True pastors are God-appointed, not self-appointed. It is the Holy Spirit who selects those who are to serve in pastoral ministry, and He plants each pastor where He chooses (*see* Acts 20:28). According to First Corinthians 12:18, who should determine where *you* are to be placed in the Body of Christ (the church where you attend and serve)? Is this true in your life?

2. As a believer, when God looks at you, He sees you as *righteous* in Christ (*see* 2 Corinthians 5:21). What does Psalm 92:12-15 say you can expect to see happening in and through your life? What do you need to do in order to see these wonderful things take place (*see* verse 13)?

3. Again and again, we have seen that the primary responsibility of a pastor is to feed God's people the truth of Scripture. According to the following verses, what does the Bible say will happen when you feed on God's Word? What is *your part* in the process?
   • Psalm 119:11,105
   • Acts 20:32
   • Hebrews 4:12
   • Jeremiah 23:28,29
   • James 1:21
   • 2 Timothy 3:16,17

PRACTICAL APPLICATION

But be ye doers of the word, and not hearers only,
deceiving your own selves.
— James 1:22

In the New Testament, the word for "church" is the Greek word *ekklesia*. It depicts *the body of believers who have been called out, called forth, selected, and assembled to be God's representatives in every town, city, state or nation; a body called to make decisions that affect the atmosphere of the region in which they lived.*

1. As a believer, you are a part of the Church — the *ekklesia*. How does the meaning of this word expand your understanding of God's purpose for the Church?

2. The Athenians who were selected to serve in the *ekklesia* in Athens considered it a high honor. Do you consider it an honor to be a part of the Church? Why or why not?

3. In what ways are you actively *being* the Church and fulfilling the meaning of *ekklesia*?

4. In what areas are you falling short and need the Holy Spirit to empower you to come up higher?

TOPIC

God's Reward for Pastors

SCRIPTURES

1. **Ephesians 4:11** — And he gave some, apostles; and some, prophets; and some, evangelists; and some, pastors and teachers.

2. **1 Peter 5:1-4** — The elders which are among you I exhort, who am also an elder, and a witness of the sufferings of Christ, and also a partaker of the glory that shall be revealed: Feed the flock of God which is among you, taking the oversight thereof, not by constraint, but willingly [according to God]; not for filthy lucre, but of a ready mind; Neither as being lords over God's heritage, but being ensamples to

the flock. And when the chief Shepherd shall appear, ye shall receive a crown of glory that fadeth not away.

GREEK WORDS

1. "pastors" — ποιμήν (*poimen*): a shepherd; pictures one who tends, rules, governs, feeds, guards, guides, and protects a flock

2. "elders" — πρεσβύτερος (*presbuteros*): depicts the spiritual representatives of Israel, such as ruling members of local synagogues or teachers of the Law who publicly taught in synagogues; such elders were deemed worthy of honor due to their positions; pictures those who have legal or spiritual authority; officially appointed church leaders

3. "exhort" — παρακαλέω (*parakaleo*): to encourage; to exhort; to console someone else; a military term meaning to stir troops to action; to pray or beg; an appeal intended to ignite a hearer to action

4. "feed" — ποιμήν (*poimen*): it is a direct command; to do the work of a shepherd; tend, rule, govern, feed, guard, guide, and protect the flock

5. "flock" — ποίμνιον (*poimnion*): a flock of sheep; a congregation

6. "taking the oversight" — ἐπίσκοπος (*episkopos*): to administrate or manage; pictures a supervisory position; one whose responsibility is to guide, direct, and give oversight; a bishop

7. "constraint" — ἀναγκαστῶς (*anagkastos*): compulsion; by force; against one's will

8. "willingly" — ἑκουσίως (*hekousios*): willingly; of one's free will; of one's own accord

9. "according to God" — κατὰ Θεόν (*kata Theon*): being answerable to God

10. "filthy lucre" — αἰσχροκερδῶς (*aischrokerdos*): shameful gain; pictures a dirty game of cards; shamefully throwing dice to make a gain; implying that the task is no more than a game to be played for financial gain

11. "ready mind" — προθύμως (*prothumos*): enthusiastically; eager; ready to do

12. "being lords" — κατακυριεύω (*katakurieuo*): compound of κατά (*kata*) and κυριεύω (*kurieuo*); the word κατά (*kata*) carries the idea of a force that is dominating or subjugating, and the word κυριεύω (*kurieuo*) pictures the force of a lord or master; compounded, to completely conquer, to master, to quash, to crush, to subdue, to defeat,

to force into a humiliating submission, or to bring one to his knees in surrender; domineering; pictures a tyrant-type of person

13. "ensamples" — τύπος (*tupos*): an example; pictures a permanent impression; a copy; an image; a pattern; a model for others to follow; a pattern for others to see and imitate

14. "Chief Shepherd" — ἀρχιποίμην (*archipoimen*): the chief shepherd; the head shepherd; the arch-shepherd; in context, Jesus Christ as the Chief Shepherd

SYNOPSIS

Hopefully it is becoming clear just how important pastors are when it comes to the ongoing care and spiritual growth of God's people. They are one of the fivefold gifts given to build and strengthen the Church. As we have seen in Ephesians 4:11, our anchor verse, the apostle Paul said, "And he [Jesus] gave some, apostles; and some, prophets; and some, evangelists; and some, pastors and teachers."

Did you notice the word "some," which is repeated four times in this verse? Its recurring appearance emphasizes the fact that Jesus gave us *some* — not many, but some — apostles, prophets, evangelists, pastors, and teachers. Contrary to what you may have heard, these gifts are not in abundance; they are rare in their occurrence. In other words, finding a good pastor is an exceptional blessing.

We saw that the word "pastor" in Ephesians 4:11 is the Greek word *poimen* — the very word for *a shepherd*. It pictures *one who tends, rules, governs, feeds, guards, guides, and protects a flock*. We saw in our last lesson that pastors are handpicked by God to oversee the most prestigious people on the planet — the Church. They are to first feed themselves and care for their spiritual needs; then they are to feed and care for the spiritual needs of God's people entrusted to them.

The emphasis of this lesson:

Peter exhorted pastors to feed God's people the spiritual nourishment of Scripture and oversee their spiritual development with a good attitude. Financial gain should never be the aim of any pastor. Those who obediently and faithfully carry out God's will, He will reward.

Peter 'Exhorted' His Fellow Pastors

Peter was a pastor in the New Testament Church, and in First Peter 5:1, he spoke specifically to his fellow pastors and said, "The elders which are among you I exhort, who am also an elder, and a witness of the sufferings of Christ, and also a partaker of the glory that shall be revealed."

Notice that Peter called himself an "elder." In Greek, this is the word *presbuteros*, which is where we get the words *presbyter* and *Presbyterian*. This word depicts *the spiritual representatives of Israel, such as ruling members of local synagogues or teachers of the Law who publicly taught in synagogues*. Such elders were deemed worthy of honor due to their God-given positions. The word *presbuteros* also pictures *those who have legal or spiritual authority* or *have been officially appointed church leaders*, which would include pastors.

In this passage, Peter identified himself as an "elder" (*presbuteros*) and then specifically took time to "exhort" the other elders among him. The word "exhort" is the Greek word *parakaleo*, which is a compound of the word *para*, meaning *to be or come alongside of*, and the word *kaleo*, meaning *to call out*. When these words are joined to form the word *parakaleo*, it pictures *one who comes right alongside of someone else and begins to call out to or plead (kaleo) with them*. It means *to encourage, to exhort*, or *to console someone else*.

Interestingly, the word *parakaleo* is also a military term, describing how commanding officers would speak encouragement to their troops and stir them to attentiveness and action. It was the equivalent of saying, "Stand tall, men! Look alive! Ready yourselves because there is a battle in front of you." Moreover, this word can also mean *to pray* or *to beg*; *it is an appeal intended to ignite a hearer to action.*

Pastors Are To Feed and Oversee God's People

After Peter "exhorted" his fellow pastors, urging them to stand tall and ready themselves for the spiritual battles ahead, he then said, "Feed the flock of God which is among you..." (1 Peter 5:2). Here again we see the word "feed" — the Greek word *poimen*, which is a direct command *to do the work of a shepherd*. This work is *to tend, rule, govern, feed, guard, guide and protect their flock* or *congregation*. Again, the primary duty of a pastor is to feed the people the teaching of the Bible.

Peter said, "Feed the flock of God which is among you, taking the oversight thereof..." (1 Peter 5:2). In Greek, the word "oversight" is the word *episkopos*, which is the same word we saw in Acts 20:28 translated as "overseers." It is a compound of the word *epi*, meaning *over*, and the word *skopos*, meaning *to look*. When these words are compounded, the new word *episkopos* means *to look over, to administrate*, or *to manage*. It pictures *one in a supervisory position whose responsibility is to guide, direct, and give oversight to the local congregation*. In the New Testament, it is the word for an *elder* or a *bishop*.

Of course, God doesn't expect perfection from pastors. He simply wants them to shepherd His people the best they can with the strength He provides. Peter said pastors are to take "…the oversight thereof, not by constraint, but willingly [according to God]…" (1 Peter 5:2). The word "constraint" here is the Greek word *anagkastos*, which describes *someone who is doing something not by compulsion, by force*, or *against his will* — or *with a bad attitude*. Rather, he is leading "willingly" — the Greek word *hekousios*, which means *willingly, of one's free will*, or *of one's own accord*.

What's interesting here is when you read this portion of Scripture in the original Greek, it includes the phrase "according to God" immediately after the word "willingly." In Greek, this is the phrase *kata Theon*, which means *answerable to God*. The implication here is that every pastor is going to be *accountable to God* regarding his pastoral duties and the attitude in which he does them. Remember, these spiritual leaders didn't appoint themselves; they were appointed by God, and therefore will be answerable to Him.

Financial Gain Should Never Be the Aim of Pastoral Ministry

Peter went on to say that elders, or spiritual overseers, were to serve "…not for filthy lucre, but of a ready mind" (1 Peter 5:2). The words "filthy lucre" is the Greek word *aischrokerdos*, and it describes *shameful gain*; *a dirty game of cards*; or *shamefully throwing dice to make a gain*. The use of this word implies that *the task of pastoring is more than a game to be played for financial gain*.

This means, when a person is called to pastoral ministry, it is not so he can make an exorbitant salary. If wealth is the aim, the person is in the wrong profession. Now there is nothing inherently wrong with receiving a sizeable salary. We saw in our first lesson that 53 percent of pastors are often concerned about their family's financial security, and only 10 percent of pastors actually retire from ministry. So churches should generously take care of their pastors to alleviate financial pressure. At the same time, big money should never be the ambition of a pastor or anyone else serving in ministry.

Jesus is the Good Shepherd, and as our example, He laid down His life for us, His sheep (*see* John 10:11). The only profit He looked forward to receiving through His obedience was knowing that He pleased the father by fulfilling His will (*see* John 17:4) and seeing people make it to Heaven who would believe on Him as the Son of God and Savior of the world. Pastoral ministry is all about *giving*, not getting.

Rather than filthy lucre being the motivator, Peter said it should be "a ready mind." In Greek, the words "ready mind" is *prothumos*, and it means *to be enthusiastically willing or eager; ready to do*. The role of a pastor is an assignment given by Heaven. Thus, it is a privilege to serve God's people as a shepherd (*poimen*), an overseer (*episkopos*), or an elder (*presbuteros*). Pastoral ministry is one of great influence, and those called by God to serve in this capacity should be eager and enthusiastic about it.

Pastors Are To Be Good Examples for Others To Imitate

Peter went on to say, "Neither as being lords over God's heritage, but being ensamples to the flock" (1 Peter 5:3). The phrase "being lords" is the Greek word *katakurieuo*, which is a compound of the words *kata* and *kurieuo*. The word *kata* carries the idea of *a force that is dominating or subjugating*, and the word *kurieuo* pictures *the force of a lord or master*. When these words are compounded to form *katakurieuo*, it means *to completely conquer, to master, to quash, to crush, to subdue, to defeat, to force into a humiliating submission, or to bring one to his knees in surrender*. It denotes *a domineering influence* and pictures *a tyrant-type of person*. So when Peter said, "Neither as being lords over God's heritage," he was saying, "As pastors, don't be domineering tyrants that crush your congregations."

Instead, he said be "...ensamples to the flock" (1 Peter 5:3). The word "ensamples" is the Greek word *tupos*, and it describes *an example; a permanent impression; a copy; an image; a pattern; a model for others to follow; a pattern for others to see and imitate*. The fact of the matter is a person in pastoral ministry is being watched all the time. Their life is a living sermon.

If you're a spiritual leader, your life is preaching all the time whether you recognize it or not. People watch how you speak to your spouse, how you react in difficult situations, how you give and spend your money, how you pray, and how you worship. You're on an invisible platform at all times, and your life is an example to people. In many ways, when you're pastoring or serving in spiritual leadership, your ministry never stops.

At this point it must be said that there are no perfect pastors. If you're looking for one, give up your search. Just as there are no perfect sheep, neither is there a perfect pastor. All of us are imperfect human beings. The only One who is perfect is Jesus, and those who obediently and faithfully carry out His will, He will reward.

To the pastors who take their calling seriously and serve with excellence, Peter said, "When the chief Shepherd shall appear, ye shall receive a crown of glory that fadeth not away" (1 Peter 5:4). The phrase "chief Shepherd" in Greek is *archipoimen*, and it describes *the chief shepherd, the head shepherd,* or *the arch-shepherd.* Jesus is the Chief Shepherd — the greatest Shepherd and Shepherd of all shepherds. One day He is going to appear before us, and to the pastors who have carried out their jobs faithfully, He is going to give a special crown. This is both the greatest motivation and highest reward for obediently serving Him in pastoral ministry.

In our final lesson, we will look at Jesus' ultimate example of a good shepherd and explore seven signals Jesus gave to help you recognize the voice of your pastor.

STUDY QUESTIONS

**Study to shew thyself approved unto God, a workman that needeth not to be ashamed, rightly dividing the word of truth.
— 2 Timothy 2:15**

1. Pastors are not the only ones who will have their works examined. One day the lives of each and every believer will be examined by Jesus Himself. What does the Bible say about this in Romans 14:10-12; Second Corinthians 5:9,10; and Hebrews 4:13?

2. Jesus said, "Behold, I come quickly; and my reward is with me, to give every man according as his work shall be" (Revelation 22:12). What did the apostle Paul say about the testing of our works in First Corinthians 3:12-15? How will Jesus evaluate what we are 'building' in this

life? (Also consider First Corinthians 9:24-27; Second Timothy 4:8; James 1:12; and Revelation 3:11.)

PRACTICAL APPLICATION

> But be ye doers of the word, and not hearers only,
> deceiving your own selves.
> — James 1:22

1. More than likely, you have watched the lives of those in spiritual leadership — many times without thinking. Can you recall seeing your pastor or a spiritual leader handling a difficult situation in a godly manner? Describe what took place — including his attitude and response — and how it helped you in your personal walk with God.

2. Just as people are observing pastors, they are also watching you. Once someone knows you're a Christian, they're watching to see how you live your life. Has anyone ever told you that the way you handled a situation impacted them in a positive way? If so, take a moment and share what took place and how it affected the person watching.

LESSON 5

TOPIC

God's Choice for a Pastor To Feed You

SCRIPTURES

1. **John 10:11** — I am the good shepherd: the good shepherd giveth his life for the sheep.

2. **John 10:3-5** — ...The sheep hear his voice: and he calleth his own sheep by name, and leadeth them out. And when he putteth forth his own sheep, he goeth before them, and the sheep follow him: for they know his voice. And a stranger will they not follow, but will flee from him: for they know not the voice of strangers.

GREEK WORDS

1. "the good shepherd" — ὁ ποιμὴν ὁ καλός (*ho poimen ho kalos*): ὁ ποιμὴν (*ho poimen*) refers to THE shepherd — the feeder, protector, and ruler of a flock of men; ὁ καλός (*ho kalos*) refers to THE good one; the most excellent one; the one who is the supreme example

2. "giveth" — τίθημι (*tithemi*): to set in place; to position; to fix; to establish

3. "life" — ψυχή (*psuche*): soul; mind, will, and emotions; hence, all that one is

4. "for" — ὑπὲρ (*huper*): on behalf of

5. "sheep" — πρόβατον (*probaton*): used to depict sheep in the New Testament

6. "hear" — ἀκούω (*akouo*): hear; comprehend; perceive; recognize; where we get the word acoustics

7. "his voice" — τῆς φωνῆς αὐτοῦ (*tes phones autou*): with a definite article, THE voice of him; his voice; implies a clearly recognizable voice of their own unique shepherd

8. "calleth" — φωνέω (*phoneo*): to give a sound, signal, or hearable call

9. "his own sheep" — τὰ ἴδια πρόβατα (*ta idia probata*): his own unique sheep; those that are peculiarly his sheep

10. "by name" — κατ᾽ ὄνομα (*kat' onoma*): according to their name; by name; implies relationship, as he knows their name

11. "leadeth…out" — ἐξάγω (*exago*): to lead out; to lead out of a harmful environment; to lead out into better pastures

12. "before them" — ἔμπροσθεν αὐτῶν (*emprosthen auton*): in front of; before you; before the face, not behind you; pictures leadership; one who goes before and visibly leads others

13. "follow" — ἀκολουθέω (*akoloutheo*): to follow; to go somewhere with a person; to accompany another person on a trip; to tirelessly accompany someone; to constantly be at the side of an individual; to always be in close proximity with a person; to follow like a traveling companion; to follow after someone or something in a very determined and purposeful manner

14. "know" — οἶδα (*oida*): to see, perceive, understand, or comprehend; confident knowledge gained by personal experience or personal observation

15. "stranger" — ἀλλότριος (*allotrios*): foreign; alien; different; strange; unfamiliar; unknown
16. "will…not" — οὐ μὴ (*ou me*): double negative; no, never; literally, in no way not
17. "but" — ἀλλά (*alla*): a break in thought that means "on the contrary"
18. "flee" — φεύγω (*pheugo*): to flee; to take flight; to run away; to run as fast as possible; to escape; pictures one's feet flying as he runs from a situation
19. "from" — ἀπ' (*ap'*): away from; to put space between oneself and someone or something else; implies distance
20. "for" — ὅτι (*hoti*): expresses purpose; because; for the explicit reason
21. "not" — οὐκ (*ouk*): emphatically; absolutely not

SYNOPSIS

In our first lesson, we saw many alarming statistics regarding pastors and the many challenges they face as they serve in ministry. Then in our second lesson, we excavated Ezekiel 34 and got a good picture of God's expectation of pastors, including seven specific responsibilities they are called to fulfill. In our third lesson, we unpacked Acts 20:28 and examined God's charge to pastors throughout the ages. And in our last lesson, we learned that God has a reward especially for pastors. One day, not too long from now, Jesus the Chief Shepherd is coming, and when He appears, He will give a crown of glory to every pastor who obediently carried out God's will and did it with a right attitude.

The emphasis of this lesson:

Jesus is the Good Shepherd and the supreme example of what a pastor should be. Not only are you His sheep, you're also a sheep of an earthly pastor. Jesus said you can recognize your pastor's voice and will be supernaturally drawn to him. It's a divine connection like no other.

How Did Jesus Describe a Good Pastor?

In John chapter 10, Jesus took time to describe pastoral ministry, and in verse 11 He made this stunning declaration: "I am the good shepherd; the good shepherd giveth his life for the sheep." There are several words in this passage that are very important to understand, including the phrase "the good shepherd." In Greek, it is *ho poimen ho kalos*: the words *ho poimen* refer to *THE shepherd — the feeder, protector, and ruler of a flock of men*; the words *ho kalos* refer to *THE good one*; *the most excellent one*; *the one who is the supreme example.*

In the original Greek, the first part of this verse literally says, "I am THE Shepherd, THE Good One." This is Jesus Himself lifting His voice declaring that He is the Best One, or the best, most superior example of a shepherd. Again, the word "shepherd" is the Greek word *poimen*, which describes *one who feeds, tends, guards, guides, and protects a flock or congregation*. The word *kalos* describes *one that is superior* or *one that is excellent, the best, above and beyond all others.*

Next, notice the word "giveth." Here it is a form of the Greek word *tithemi*, which means *to place, to lay down,* or *to establish*. It is the same word we saw translated as "hath made" in Acts 20:28. By using this word, Jesus is letting us know that as the Good Shepherd, His life was *established* for one purpose — His pastoral ministry was *set in place* by God *to lay down* His life for the sheep. Similarly, that is also what a good shepherd — or a good pastor — does for the people he pastors. He lays down his life in order *to establish* them in the principles of God's Word.

Jesus was the supreme example of what a pastor should be. He held nothing back but gave His life for us, His sheep. Interestingly, the word "life" here is not *bios*, which means *physical life*, or *zoe*, which describes *spiritual life*. In this verse, the word "life" is the Greek word *psuche*, which is where we get the words *psyche* and *psychology*. It describes *the mind, the will, and the emotions* or **all** that a person is. Like Jesus, a good pastor dedicates the fullness of his life — his mind, will, and emotions — to his God-given responsibilities.

This brings us to the word "for." When Jesus said "…The good shepherd giveth his life *for* the sheep," the word "for" is the Greek word *huper*, which means *on behalf of*. Hence, a good pastor is one who gives, invests, or lays down his life *on behalf of* others. In Greek, the word "sheep" is *probaton*, and it is used to describe *sheep in the New Testament*, which is the Church.

Ultimately, Jesus gave His life for us. Of His own free will, He laid it down and surrendered to the will of the Father. But He didn't just suffer horrific beatings and endure the death of the Cross to pardon our sins. He sacrificed His life in order to establish us on a good foundation of faith, and that should be the goal of every pastor.

As a Sheep, You Can Recognize
the Voice of Your Pastor

When we look at the earlier verses in John chapter 10, we find Jesus giving us principals on how we can recognize the voice of our earthly shepherd or pastor. He said, "...The sheep hear his voice: and he calleth his own sheep by name, and leadeth them out" (John 10:3).

Note the word "hear." It is the Greek word *akouo*, which means *to hear, to comprehend, to perceive, or to recognize*. It's where we get the word *acoustics*. Jesus said the sheep hear "his voice," which in the original Greek actually says *tēs phōnēs autou*. Here we see the definite article is included, which means this part of the verse would literally be translated, "The sheep hear THE voice of Him; his voice." This implies a clearly recognizable voice of their own unique shepherd. In other words, all of us are able to perceive, distinguish, and recognize our shepherd's voice above all other voices.

Take, for example, the voice of Rick Renner. He is called by God to be a pastor, but he is not called to be everyone's pastor. Nevertheless, the people he *is* called to pastor — in Moscow and around the world through the media — are able to hear his voice. They're attracted to his teaching, they have a sincere love and appreciation for him, and they want to follow him. At the same time, there are other people who are just not able to "hear" Rick. In other words, they are not drawn to him, they are unable to receive revelation from him, and they have no interest in following him. They are attracted to the voice of another pastor and are able to recognize and hear his voice, and that is perfectly all right.

Basically, no pastor is everybody's pastor. A person can only be a pastor to those who recognize his voice. Again, there are some people who tune into Rick's TV program, and they don't get anything out of it. Then there are others who tune in and are hanging on every word; they just can't seem to get enough. Why? It is because God has created a unique relationship between a pastor and those called to be his sheep. In this case, the viewers are able to hear Rick's voice, and he is able to speak into their life. It's a divine spiritual connection. Sheep are able to hear and receive from the shepherd designed to lead them.

A Shepherd Calls His Sheep and Leads Them Out

Jesus went on to say that a good shepherd "…calleth his own sheep by name…" (John 10:3). The word "calleth" is the Greek word *phoneo*, which means *to give a sound, signal, or hearable call*. In other words, believers are able to clearly hear the voice of the one who has authority to speak into their life. And each shepherd, or pastor, calls "his own sheep," which in Greek indicates *his own unique sheep* or *those that are peculiarly his sheep.* The phrase "by name" is *kat' onoma* in Greek, and it means *according to their name* or *by name.* It implies *relationship*, as he knows and is familiar with their name.

Once a pastor calls those sheep with whom he is in relationship, the Bible says he "…leadeth them out" (John 10:3). In Greek, the words "leadeth out" is *exago*, and it means *to lead out; to lead out of a harmful environment; to lead out into better pastures.*

Sheep Tirelessly Follow Their Shepherd

In John 10:4, Jesus continued to describe the actions of a good shepherd saying, "And when he putteth forth his own sheep, he goeth before them, and the sheep follow him: for they know his voice." The phrase "before them" in Greek is *emprosthen auton*, which means *in front of; before you; before the face, not behind you.* It pictures leadership; one who goes before and visibly leads others. This indicates that the pastor is out in front of his sheep leading the way, and they are willing to "follow."

In Greek, the word "follow" is the word *akoloutheo*, which means *to follow; to go somewhere with a person; to accompany another person on a trip.* It carries the idea of *tirelessly accompanying someone; to constantly be at the side of an individual;* or *to always be in close proximity with a person.* It is the picture of *one following someone like a traveling companion.* Furthermore, it means *to follow after someone or something in a very determined and purposeful manner.*

The spiritual connection you have with your pastor is supernaturally unique. God gives you an innate desire to follow him on a spiritual journey — to be right at his side, hearing what he has to say. He has authority to speak into your life, and you are well able to recognize his voice.

Sheep Confidently Know and Recognize Their Shepherd's Voice

The Bible says as one of his sheep, you "know his voice" (John 10:4). The word "know" in Greek is *oida*, which means *to see, perceive, understand, or comprehend*. It denotes *a confident knowledge gained by personal experience or personal observation*. What can you confidently perceive and comprehend? Jesus said "his voice," which is the Greek phrase *tes phones autou* — the exact phrase we saw in verse 3. Again, it includes a definite article, indicating *THE voice of him; his voice*. It implies that sheep hear *the clearly recognizable voice of their own unique shepherd*.

In John 10:5, Jesus went on to say, "And a stranger will they not follow, but will flee from him: for they know not the voice of strangers." The word "stranger" is the Greek word *allotrios*, which means *foreign; alien; different; strange; unfamiliar*, or *unknown*. Sheep *will not* follow a stranger. The words "will...not" is a very strong, double negative that literally means *no, never, in no way not*. "Follow" is again the Greek word *akoloutheo*, meaning *to follow* or *to go somewhere with a person; to tirelessly accompany someone* and *to constantly be at their side*. In this case, the sheep will *never, in no way* follow or accompany a stranger (one who is not their shepherd).

Interestingly, even the word "but" — the Greek word *alla* — is significant. It describes a break in thought that means *"on the contrary."* Instead of tirelessly following a foreigner or alien, *on the contrary*, they will "flee from him." The word "flee" in Greek is *pheugo*, which means *to flee; to take flight; to run away*. It denotes *a person running as fast as possible* and pictures *one's feet flying as he runs from a situation*. The word "from" in Greek is the word *ap'*, which means *away from; to put space between oneself and someone or something else*; it implies *distance*. This means, if sheep are in the pasture of another shepherd, they will have a strong desire to get away from that individual and get back with the shepherd they are supposed to be with.

Why will sheep want to leave? The Bible says, "...For they know not the voice of strangers" (John 10:5). The word "for" here is the Greek word *hoti*, which expresses *purpose* and would better be translated as *because*. Sheep will naturally want to get away *for the explicit reason* that they "know not the voice of strangers." The word "know" here is again the Greek word *oida*, but in this case, it is preceded by the word "not," which means *emphatically; absolutely not*. Thus, sheep will *absolutely not* follow or want to stay connected to "strangers" — again, the Greek word *allotrios*, describing *a foreigner or alien.* The reason is that they emphatically don't perceive, understand, comprehend, or have personal experience with that individual.

Seven Signals To Recognize the Voice of Your Pastor

Taking the meaning of all these words from Jesus into account, we can identify seven specific signals to help you clearly recognize the voice of your pastor — the one who has God-given authority and responsibility to speak into your life.

Signal #1: You will have a spiritual connection to him.

Signal #2: You will have a desire to hear more from him. Because of the divine connection God has established, you will want to hear his voice and receive what he is saying.

Signal #3: You will have a sense of security by being under his ministry. You will know that you're in the right place because you'll feel safe under his leadership.

Signal #4: You will have a supernatural desire to honor him. When a person has that God-given authority to be your pastor or speak into your life, you'll have a desire to honor that individual.

Signal #5: You will have a drawing to follow his leadership. Internally, it will feel as though you want to stick closely to your pastor and "follow" him on a spiritual journey so that he can continue to speak into your life.

Signal #6: You will have a desire to serve alongside him. When you are divinely called to be under someone's spiritual authority, you will want to help him in whatever way you can.

Signal #7: You will have a willingness to be corrected by him if needed. Shepherds sometimes have to bring correction to their sheep, which is something no one really wants to receive. But if God gives you a willingness to receive correction, it is a sure signal that you are connected with the person God selected to speak into your life.

These are seven signals to help you recognize the voice of your pastor or the one that has God-given authority to speak into your life. Remember, our best example of pastor is Jesus — the Chief Shepherd of all shepherds. Take time to pray for your pastor and honor him for the special gift he is in your life.

STUDY QUESTIONS

Study to shew thyself approved unto God, a workman that
needeth not to be ashamed, rightly dividing the word of truth.
— 2 Timothy 2:15

1. In John 10:3-5, Jesus gave seven specific signals to help you recognize
    the voice of your pastor — the one who is called by God to speak into
    your life. Carefully reflect on these seven signals. How do they help
    you better understand and appreciate the relationship you have with
    your pastor? Which of these can you actually see operating in your
    life?

2. The Bible tells us to honor our spiritual leaders, which includes our
    pastors (*see* 1 Timothy 5:17). Take a few moments to answer the fol-
    lowing questions in order to evaluate the level of honor you are giving
    to your pastor.

    *   How would you describe your attendance: *regular, random*, or *seldom?*

    *   How about your punctuality? Are you usually *a little early, on time*,
        or *late?*

    *   How often would you say you pray for your pastor and his family:
        often, sometimes, or *never?*

    *   How would you describe your words about your pastor to others?
        Positive and supportive or *negative and critical?*

    *   When your pastor is teaching, are you *leaning in and taking in* what
        he's saying, or is your mind *preoccupied with other things?*

    *   If your pastor asks the congregation — which includes you — for
        help in a certain area, do you *look for ways you can help*, or do you
        look for excuses to exempt yourself from having to help?

3. In light of your answers, would you say that you are *honoring* your pas-
    tor by your actions or *dishonoring* him? If you answered dishonoring,
    take time now to repent and ask God to forgive you and give you a
    heart of honor for the person He has provided to be your shepherd.

PRACTICAL APPLICATION

But be ye doers of the word, and not hearers only,
deceiving your own selves.
— James 1:22

The Bible says, "…Be mindful to be a blessing, especially to those of the household of faith [those who belong to God's family with you, the believers]" (Galatians 6:10 *AMPC*). Pause for a moment and ask yourself, *Is my mind full of ways to be a blessing to those of the household of faith — including my pastor?*

1. When was the last time you sent your pastor a quick handwritten note of thanks? Why not take a little time this week and write him or her a *thank you* note. And while you're at it, attach a gift card to one of his favorite places to eat or shop. Remember, what you plant you will reap, and as you refresh others, you too will be refreshed (*see* Galatians 6:7; Proverbs 11:25).

2. Another wonderful way to bless your pastor and his family is by *praying* for them. First Timothy 2:1-3 says you are to pray for those in authority, which includes your pastor. Take time now to ask God to pour out His blessings of wisdom, peace, provision, protection, favor, boldness, direction, and joy on your pastor and his family. Bless his marriage and relationships with unity and peace, and pray that strife and division would be bound. Bless His personal relationship with Jesus with fresh revelation of truth and the anointing of the Holy Spirit.

Notes

Notes